JOEY AND PATCHES:
The STORY of Two kittens

by MARGARET S. JOHNSON

and HELEN LOSSING JOHNSON

Illustrated by MARGARET S. JOHNSON

Originally published in 1947
Cover illustration by Victoria Skakandi and Margaret S. Johnson
Cover design by Kayla Ellingsworth
© 2021 Jenny Phillips
goodandbeautiful.com

One stormy September night, two small kittens were huddled together under an old farm wagon. The rain was falling in torrents, and the wind was blowing hard. The kittens mewed and mewed, but no answer came, and after a while, they kept quiet.

Early that morning, the kittens, who were about six weeks old, had followed their mother when she went to hunt mice in the field. Their little gray sister was with them, and they all played happily around the big haystack.

When the mother cat started for home, the little gray sister went with her. But the two kittens, whose names were Joey and Patches, were having such fun running in and out of an old woodchuck hole that they did not notice that their mother and sister had left them. After a while they grew tired, so they curled up in the hole and went to sleep.

When Joey and Patches woke up, they were very hungry. They began to mew for their mother, but she was nowhere to be seen. The sky was getting dark and cloudy, and the wind was blowing. The kittens mewed louder and began to run through the grass as fast as their short legs could go.

They had never been away from their mother before, and they did not know how to get home. They ran in the wrong direction, and when the rain began to fall, they were farther away from home. Their soft fur was getting soaked, but they put back their little ears and struggled along until they came to another haystack. Close to the haystack was an old farm wagon, and Joey and Patches ran under it and snuggled down on some hay where the rain could not touch them.

Toward morning the storm cleared away, but the kittens did not come out from under the wagon. They were lost and frightened and hungry, and when the daylight came, they began to cry again.

Suddenly they heard something coming through the grass, and they jumped up with happy little mews, for they thought it was their mother. But when they saw a brown and white dog coming toward them, they were frightened. They fluffed up their tails, and arched their little backs, and tried to look very fierce. When the big spaniel saw them, he wagged his tail and looked at them with a friendly expression in his eyes.

Soon a man appeared, and he stopped when he saw the dog looking under the wagon. "What have you got there, Flash?" he said. And Patches and Joey mewed and ran toward the man.

"What beautiful kittens!" he exclaimed in surprise. "I wonder where they came from." Then he stooped down and picked them up. Both kittens began to purr, and the man, whose name was Mr. Kent, started back to his house with Joey and Patches in his arms.

Mr. Kent's wife was in the kitchen, and he put the kittens down on the floor beside her. "Here are two hungry babies," he said, and Mrs. Kent quickly warmed some milk and gave Joey and Patches a saucer full of it.

Then the kittens began to lap it up with their little pink tongues. They were so hungry that they stuck their noses in the milk and sneezed and choked and got their whiskers all milky.

When they finished drinking, they tried to wash their faces with their soft paws. But their mother had always washed them, and they could not do it very well. So they went over to a rug and curled up close together. Soon they were fast asleep.

Both kittens were beautiful, and Mr. and Mrs. Kent wanted to keep them. Patches' silvery gray coat was marked with velvety black stripes and patches; his paws and chest were white. Joey was pale gray, with dark gray stripes, and his paws and chest were white, too.

While the kittens slept, Mr. and Mrs. Kent found that they belonged on the next farm,

but the people did not want them. So Mr. and
Mrs. Kent decided to keep Joey and Patches.
When the kittens woke up, they began to play,
rolling over and over and chasing each other
all around the kitchen. Patches was much
more gentle than Joey, and sometimes he
mewed when Joey bit him too hard.

Suddenly they stopped playing and looked toward the kitchen door. A big striped cat stood there, and Patches ran toward it, for the cat looked like his mother. Joey followed, and they had almost reached the cat when it gave an angry hiss and growl. Patches stopped so suddenly that Joey bumped into him and pushed him against the old cat, whose name was Tawney.

Tawney's big yellow eyes gleamed angrily, and he lifted his paw to strike Patches. But Patches rolled over with a soft little "*Purr-ow*," and Tawney jumped up on a chair and sat there, looking crossly at the kittens.

They wanted to play with Tawney, and they tried to get hold of his long tail. At last Tawney jumped down off the chair and ran upstairs. After that, Joey and Patches were kept shut up in the kitchen, and they did not see Tawney again for a long time.

But Flash, the big spaniel, often came in the kitchen, and the kittens loved him. They would rub against his legs, and Flash would sniff at them, wagging his short tail. When he lay down, Joey and Patches played with his paws and his tail. Patches never stuck out his claws, but Joey sometimes bit and scratched, and then the big dog growled. But Joey was not afraid, for he knew Flash would not hurt him.

*B*y the time the kittens were three months old, Mrs. Kent let them play all over the house. At first they were afraid of the stairs, but soon they found that it was great fun to scamper up and down them. They loved to race each other to the sofa; then the first kitten to get under the sofa would keep the other one out.

Patches thought that the bathtub was a
delightful place. If the tap was dripping, he
tried to catch the drops of water, and he would
tip his head and watch with puzzled eyes
when the drops disappeared down the drain.

One day Mrs. Kent could not find Joey and

Patches. She went all over the house calling them, but they did not come. At last she went into the guest room and found the closet door open. On the closet floor were the kittens, fast asleep on her best dress. The furry little rascals had been climbing up all the clothes and had pulled down Mrs. Kent's dress.

Mrs. Kent was annoyed because her dress was mussed up, so she put the kittens out in the yard and shut the door.

Patches and Joey had not been out of doors since Mr. Kent found them, and the world looked big and strange to them. They crouched down on the kitchen porch and looked out into the bright October sunshine.

Patches' green eyes and Joey's deep yellow ones grew big and round with excitement when they saw Flash coming toward them. They were so glad to see their dog friend that they ran out to greet him, and soon they were playing in the sunshine.

After this, the kittens played in the yard every fine day, and before long they found their way to the barn. In the evenings they watched Mr. Kent when he milked the cows, and they soon learned to expect a saucer of warm milk.

Patches wanted everyone to love him, and

he tried to make friends with Tawney. The old cat would sometimes let Patches lie on the sofa beside him.

Joey loved to tease Tawney by jumping out from behind chairs and doors at him, so Tawney did not like Joey.

One afternoon, Mr. and Mrs. Kent drove to town. They thought that both kittens were shut in the kitchen, but Joey was asleep under the sofa in the living room. Soon he woke up and began climbing up the chairs and sofa.

His sharp claws pulled out pieces of the plush which covered the chairs, and Joey thought this was great fun. By the time he grew tired, one chair was scratched all over, and another was torn.

Suddenly Joey noticed an aquarium on a table near a window. The sun was shining into it, and the beautiful goldfish gleamed brightly. Joey scrambled up on a chair and jumped to the table. His yellow eyes were shining, and he struck at the fish. But he hit the glass and drew back in surprise. Then he put his paws on the edge of the aquarium and tried to sniff at the fish. The water tickled his nose and made him sneeze, and he slapped at it with his paws. He pulled out some of the plants and splashed water on the table.

When Mr. and Mrs. Kent came home, Joey

was asleep in the living room and Patches was in the kitchen.

Mrs. Kent was so angry with Joey for pulling the plants out of the aquarium and tearing the chairs that she said he would have to live in the barn. So Mr. Kent put Joey in an empty stall with hay to lie on, and he gave him some warm milk and meat.

Joey went to sleep after he ate his supper. When he woke up a few hours later, the barn was dark. He rolled over and stretched out his paws, thinking that he was in the kitchen with Patches. But no warm, furry little brother mewed softly to him, and Joey jumped up and ran to the barn door. When he found it was shut, he sat down and mewed loudly. At last he was too tired to mew any more, and he went back to the stall and fell asleep.

Patches was unhappy, too. All his life he had slept close to Joey, and he felt lost without him.

Mrs. Kent kept Patches shut in the house for a week. He sat in a chair by the window, and Joey jumped up on the sill outside, and they tried to touch each other through the glass.

Once Joey climbed upon a grape arbor near the back door and jumped across to a bedroom window. Mrs. Kent was surprised when she found him in the room; it was such a long jump from the arbor, she could hardly believe Joey had made it.

The next evening Patches rushed out of the door when Mr. Kent went out. Joey was on the back porch, and the two kittens ran off to some woods nearby. It was getting dark, and Mr. Kent did not notice them.

For a while the kittens had great fun, racing through the underbrush and chasing each other a little way up the trees.

Suddenly they stopped playing and listened. Something was running through the woods, and soon Joey and Patches saw a strange dog coming toward them.

The frightened kittens quickly climbed a tree, and when the dog looked up and barked at them, they kept going higher and higher.

After a while the dog went away, but the kittens did not come down. They had never been up so high before, and the ground looked far away.

Joey and Patches

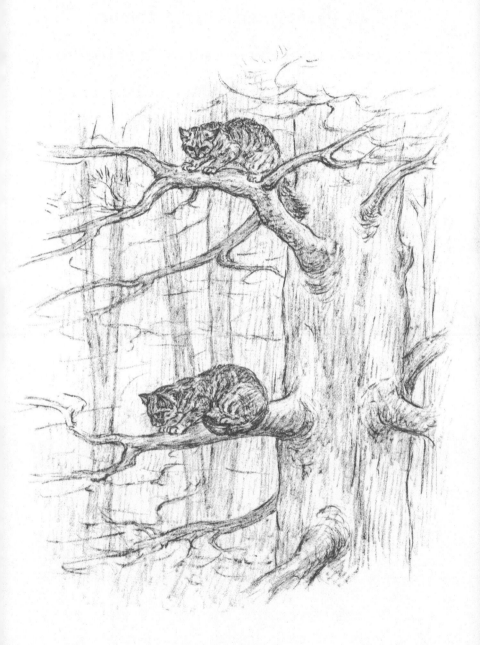

An hour went by, and Joey and Patches began to feel cold. Patches was on a lower branch than Joey, and after a while he carefully crawled along to the tree trunk and started to scramble down.

But when he reached the ground, Patches did not run home. Joey was crying in the tree high above him, and he would not leave his brother. Suddenly he heard Mrs. Kent calling and ran toward her. Then he ran back to the tree and looked up. Mr. Kent turned his flashlight on the upper branches, and Joey's eyes shone as the light struck them. Mr. Kent saw that he could not get down, so he went back for a ladder. Then he carried Joey safely to the ground. Patches ran to Joey and licked his face, and he tried to follow when Mr. Kent put Joey in the barn. But Mrs. Kent took Patches to the house, and soon he was asleep in the kitchen.

*T*he two kittens loved the snow, and they
would roll in it until Patches' face and
whiskers were all white and the long hair on
Joey's hind legs was filled with tiny snowballs.

One day Patches found a piece of stale
fish in the yard. Joey rushed over to see what
he was playing with. Patches growled and

swallowed a big piece of the fish, and Joey grabbed the rest and ran off behind a bush to finish it.

That evening the kittens would not eat their supper. They looked so sick that, after supper, Mrs. Kent took them to the cat and dog doctor. He said that they were very sick kittens, and Mrs. Kent left them in the animal hospital.

Patches and Joey were put in cages next to each other and given medicine. All the next day they were too sick to eat a thing.

They were homesick and unhappy. At last
the doctor put them in a cage together, and
they felt better right away. In a few days they
were well, and Mrs. Kent came and took them
home. When they got back, they were so
happy that they raced all over the place. Then
they ran up the ladder in the hay barn and
would not come down. They wanted to sleep
there together, but Mrs. Kent took Patches in
the house.

One night Joey was out in the fields when Mr. Kent closed the barn. After a while he wandered back and sat on the kitchen porch.

Patches heard him and jumped up on a chair by the window. Suddenly Patches began to sniff, and then he sneezed. There was a smell of smoke in the house, and he did not like it. The smoke grew thicker, and he mewed loudly. Joey heard him and jumped to the window sill. In the kitchen, Patches was running around, sneezing and coughing.

Joey ran to the grape arbor and began to climb. When he reached the top, he sprang across to the bedroom window.

Mr. and Mrs. Kent were awakened by Joey's cries. Then they heard Flash barking, and they smelled smoke.

Joey followed them as they rushed downstairs. The hall was full of smoke, and Patches ran back into the kitchen when Mr. Kent opened the door. But the next instant, he saw Joey in the hall, and he leaped through the smoke to join his brother. Then the kittens ran into the living room and crouched down under the sofa.

Here Mr. Kent found them an hour later, choked and half-blinded by the smoke. Patches was licking Joey's face, while Joey licked Patches' paws.

Long after the fire had been put out and the engines had gone away, Mr. and Mrs. Kent stayed in the kitchen with Joey and Patches. The fresh, cool air coming in the open window soon revived the kittens. Now they were sleepily washing their faces after a delicious meal of liver and cream. Old Tawney looked quietly down at them from a chair, while Flash, still wide awake and excited over the fire, lay close to Mrs. Kent.

"If those kittens will go through fire and smoke to get together, they should not be parted," Mr. Kent said.

Mrs. Kent smiled as she answered. "They can sleep on the best chairs if they want to now," she said. "Joey will never be shut in the barn again."

MORE BOOKS FROM THE GOOD AND THE BEAUTIFUL LIBRARY

Toby Has a Dog and Other Books
by May Justus

Baldy the American Eagle
by Mary Adrian

Brave Little Ruby
by Shannen Yauger

Crooked Creek Ranch
by Amy Drorbaugh

GOODANDBEAUTIFUL.COM